Common Sense Management— A Biblical Perspective

Dr. R. Henry Migliore
President, Managing for Success
Professor Emeritus NSU/UCT

Managing For Success
Tulsa, Oklahoma

Common Sense Management – A Biblical Perspective
ISBN 978-0-9989006-5-0

Copyright © 2018 by R. Henry Migliore

Published by
Managing for Success
10839 S. Houston
Jenks, Oklahoma 74037
www.hmigliore.com

Printed in the United States of America.
All rights reserved under International Copyright Law.

Contents and/or cover may not be reproduced in whole or in part in any form without the express written consent of the author.

Contents

Part I: Foreword and Introduction

Foreword 2
Introduction 3

Part II: Practical Applications of Common Sense Management

Care and Feeding of the Boss 8
Care and Feeding of the Employee 11
Iceberg Theory 13
Promotion Theory 17
Managing Is Like Parenting 19
Stinger Principle 23
Cycle Theory 27
Pay Me Now or Pay Me Later 31
Afraid to Fail 35
Defensive End Theory 37
Alamo Theory: Toe the Line 39
Lawn-Mowing Theory 43
Are You Always Right? 45
Subway 47
View the World Through (Other) Colored Glasses 49
Stew In Your Own Juice 51
Snowball 53
Get Your Head Above the Clouds 55
Homeostasis 57
Seed Faith 59
Natural Rhythm 61

"I'll Be True to You While You're Gone,
    Honey Just Don't 65
Get Out of the Ghetto 67
Find Out He Is a Christian by How He Acts,
    Not by What He 69
Be the Best You Can Be 71
Never Give Up 73
Do It When It Is Important 75
Success -the Whole Person 77
Be There in the Morning 79
Excess Weight Breeds Trouble 81
Keep It Simple 83
Pine Tree 85
Failing to Prepare Is Like Preparing to Fail 87
The Product Must Be Better Than the Sales Pitch 89
The O-Ring 91
How You Use Today Determines How Tomorrow
    Uses You 97
Be Content With What You Have and Not With
    What You Are 97
Three Kinds of People 97
You Win the Race With Heart 98
Anger Is Just One Letter Away From Danger 98
The Best Kind of Pride Compels You to Do Your
    Very Best Work, Even if No One Is Watching 98
Faith Sees Where Sight Is Blind 98
Seven Days Without Prayer Makes One Weak 99
Unguided Missiles: Some Without Warheads 100
If You Are Average, You Are as Close to the Bottom
    as to the Top 100
The Only Place Success Comes Before Work Is in the
    Dictionary 100

The Indispensable Man 101
From the Lowest Depth There Is a Path to the
    Loftiest Height.. 102
Clouds That Never Rain 102
Key Man 103
My Pal, R. G. Voight.. 103
Final Mark of Success Is Humility and How You
    Are Remembered.. 103
Fess Up 104
Teamwork.. 104
Learn From the Mistakes of Others—You Cannot
    Live Long Enough to Make Them All Yourself........... 104
Do Not Learn the Tricks of the Trade Before You
    Learn the Trade 105
Nobody Knows What He Can Do Until He Tries............. 105
Noah Did Not Wait for His Ship to Come In—He
    Built One 106
The Difference Between Good and Great Is a Little
    Extra Effort... 106
The Surest Way Not to Fail Is to Determine to Succeed.... 106
It Is Easier to Keep Up Than to Catch Up......................... 107
Luck Is the Idol of the Idle 108
Working His Way Out of a Job.. 108
There Are No Second Chances for Making a First Impression
    108
Mother Teresa: A Life Not Dedicated to the Service
    of Mankind Is Useless.. 109
Success Is Never Accidental 109
Never Ask Anyone to Do Something You Would
    Not Do Yourself.. 109
The Fellow Pulling the Oars Has Little Time to
    Rock the Boat 110

Conclusion 111
Appendix A 112
Appendix B 119
Part III: Readings "Point of View" by R. Henry Migliore
Some Keys to Business Survival 126
Twenty Sure Ways to Lose Money 129
Our "Rain Forests" Are Still Shifting 132
A Look Toward the Year 2000 and the Year 2001 134
Key Plays in the Game of Life 136

About the Author 148

Part I:
Foreword and Introduction

Part I: Forward & Introduction

Foreword

Through the years I have had the opportunity to work with many organizations, conducting seminars and workshops in every area of the country. In addition, I have taught eighteen years of undergraduate and graduate classes. A key driving force for me has been the ministry of helping people to develop, teaching them to find solutions for their problems and how to become better managers in every aspect of their lives. To this end in my teaching and writing I always relate academic and business principles to practical, everyday things.

On one occasion at a seminar in Nebraska I was drawing a diagram to illustrate the "lawn-mowing theory" when a participant asked, "Why don't you write all this down?"

A few years later -here it is: *Common Sense Management With a Biblical Perspective.* I have used as a basis the greatest book ever written, the Bible, which teaches and reveals common sense.

R. Henry Migliore
October 2015

Common Sense Management—A Biblical Perspective

Introduction

Managers often tend to take themselves too seriously and to complicate matters instead of keeping them simple. Henry Migliore has avoided this, and delivers the message but succeeds in doing so without the excess of verbiage which often accompanies the subjects about which he writes. The reader is tempted to read the entire book at one sitting. This could be a mistake! Each "gem" in the book is one which should be read, then thought through and digested for later application.

While "common sense management" is an approach most of us advocate, many times there is an uncommon lack of it.

Dale D. McConkey
Professor of Management
School of Business
University of Wisconsin-Madison

Part II: Practical Applications of Common Sense Management

Part II
Practical Applications
of Common Sense Management

Part II: Practical Applications of Common Sense Management

Care, Feeding of a Boss

Part II: Practical Applications of Common Sense Management

Care and Feeding of the Boss

Almost everyone has a boss—someone who oversees and is responsible for one's activities and output. Sometimes unfortunate communication gaps exist between the boss and subordinate. Many well- managed organizations are finding various ways to dose these gaps. Every person should take the time to determine what the boss expects in specific, measurable terms.

An exercise often used in different settings is to ask a boss and one of his subordinates to list the five most important results expected by the subordinate. In a typical case, between 50 and 60 percent of the items on the lists of the people involved in the exercise are not in agreement. It could be very revealing to carry this out for yourself. I have run this exercise many times and have never had a group with more than about a 60 percent agreement. That means half the things people in organizations are working on are things the boss does not rate as important. I think that is at the root of most of management's problems. The "Care and Feeding of the Boss" theory suggests that you make up the expectation list and then reach agreement before starting. It does not make sense to work on something if you do not know where you are going, what is expected or even what is most important. The boss is "fed and happy" when he knows you agree on what is to be done and when. He is even happier when you get the desired results.

The relevant biblical principle is that of unity.

Several verses speak directly to this point. In Philippians 2:2-4, Paul is emphasizing unity of spirit and purpose, which the "Care and Feeding of the *Boss"* principle makes possible. Also

Common Sense Management—A Biblical Perspective

emphasized is the fact that the interests of others, including the boss, are crucial. The "Care and Feeding of the Boss" principle helps to bring about the state of affairs in Psalm 133:1. Those who learn what the boss expects of them will be rewarded, and those who fail to do so will be punished. (See James 4:17 on the next page.)

When I accepted the Facet Enterprises professorship at Northeastern State University/University Center (NSU/UCT) at Tulsa, Oklahoma, I made a commitment in writing as to what I hope to accomplish during the following three years. It was important that sponsoring company's Facet, TDW, Telex, and had input into what is to be accomplished. I feel confident in the fact that the officials of the sponsoring companies and NSU/UCT executives know what is to be accomplished. I report results to them three times a year.

> ... make my joy complete by being like-minded, having the same love, being one in spirit and purpose. Do nothing out of selfish ambition or vain conceit, but in humility consider others better than yourselves. Each of you should look not only to your own interests, but also to the interests of others.
> **Philippians 2:2-4 NIV**

> How good and pleasant it is when brothers (co-workers) live (and work) together in unity!
> **Psalm 133:1 NIV.**

> Anyone, then, who knows the good he ought to do and doesn't do it, sins.
> **James 4:17 NIV**

Part II: Practical Applications of Common Sense Management

Employee Care, Feeding

Common Sense Management—A Biblical Perspective

Care and Feeding of the Employee

The same "feeding of the boss" process can be utilized with employees. Let them prepare a list of what they believe they are to accomplish, while you prepare a similar list. Compare lists and negotiate. Determine and communicate the desired result in advance, and a lot of problems will take care of themselves. A key to successful "care and feeding" is to give the employee feedback on performance. Constantly reinforce positive results, and coach to correct and discourage negative results. The apostle Paul wrote:

> But this I say, He which soweth sparingly shall also sparingly; and he which soweth bountifully shall reap also bountifully.
>
> Now he that ministereth seed to the sower both minister bread for your food, and multiply your seed sown.
>
> 2 Corinthians 9:6,10

The manager who sows little time and effort with employees shall reap also sparingly from them. The manager who takes time to explain the purpose, goals, and objectives of the company and of his particular work area to the employee will help him better understand his job duties; therefore, he will be a better employee.

Part II: Practical Applications of Common Sense Management

Common Sense Management—A Biblical Perspective

Iceberg Theory

An organization, in many ways, can be likened to a vessel crossing the North Atlantic. Only a small part of an iceberg is above the water, and you cannot see the part under water. An organization, like a ship, is going somewhere. In most cases, the organization and the ship have a target -profitability in a certain market or a distant port. Both are intent on survival. You want all hands on deck. You want a systematic way to be alert for the icebergs. Anyone can see an iceberg -a janitor, a salesman, or anyone on the ship.

Strategic planning/management by objective (MBO) by its very nature encourages the communication process and gets everyone in tune with what the organization is doing. It gets all hands on deck watching for icebergs. A shipmate sees the iceberg, sounds the warning, goes to upper management -the captain of the ship -who studies the problem, sees the iceberg, sees that the whole course of the ship can be turned because of what the lowest-level member of the organization has seen. That very thing has happened in organizations with which I have worked. A salesman in the field noticed a new use for his company's product. He saw competition beginning to notice same thing. As we had set up a procedure to send information back, the firm's research and development department got hold of the new idea. Suddenly everybody in the organization was helping to get somewhere. The company made a fast entry into a new market.

The company can be thought of as in a war with other competitors, and the victory will go to the one that has the best flow of communication. Now if the chief executive officer or

Part II: Practical Applications of Common Sense Management

any supervisor does not feel that advice from a salesman or janitor is worth hearing, he is not using his people correctly, for the Bible says,

> **Only by pride cometh contention: but with the well advised is wisdom**
> (Prov. 13:10).

Therefore it seems that the "Iceberg Theory" is pretty much in line with what the Bible teaches. If a company is going to achieve its goals, it must have a continuous flow of information coming from all areas of the organization. The system of management that best achieves this is the SLRP/MBO (Strategic Long-Range Planning/Management by Objectives) system, whereby information is constantly being collected and sent upward in the hierarchy.

> **Without counsel purposes are disappointed: but in the multitude of counselors they are established.**
> Proverbs 15:22

> **Hear counsel, and receive instruction, that thou mayest be wise in thy latter end.**
> Proverbs 19:20

> **Every purpose is established by counsel....**
> Proverbs 20:18

> **For by wise counsel thou shalt make thy war: and in multitude of counsellors there is safety.**
> Proverbs 24:6

Common Sense Management—A Biblical Perspective

Part II: Practical Applications of Common Sense Management

Promotion Theory

The first advice I received when I went to work at Continental Can Company was. "If you really want to get ahead in business, the second day on the job begin training your replacement."

I did not see the point of that advice until after I had worked in organizations for a number of years, and it is this: If you are going to be promoted, you have to develop someone to take your place. I learned this lesson when a manager friend was passed over for a promotion, and later I understood why he was passed over. It would have weakened the organization. No one was available to take his place. He had not exercised "care and feeding of the employee."

It is to your advantage to develop people under you and to begin developing them quickly. If you are the only one who can do your job. when a promotion comes along. you may be passed over.

The boss may say, "You would really be good at this. but what is going to happen? No one is trained to take your place."

Many times, people are so defensive about their jobs that they do not share and help people under them develop.

They are afraid. "If I train that person, he will get my job, and I will be jobless."

Set objectives, then assist those under you in meeting these objectives.

Part II: Practical Applications of Common Sense Management

Managing's Like Parenting

Managing Is Like Parenting

Management and rearing children have much in common. I have had personal experience in both arenas for about the same period of time. Everyone believes he can do a good job until he tries it. It has taken me this long to see this theory because of experience with our children. The most difficult task I have faced is being a parent. Teaching, consulting, and writing are relatively easy. But rearing children is a difficult undertaking. Parents do not receive any formal training. They go through an evolutionary process. Children keep growing, and often, parents do not recognize the changes. Parents do the best they can but usually have little insight as to changes taking place in children's lives. I have noticed the same process in management. The organization grows through highly predictable stages. But it appears most managements are not interested in receiving training. The only time they get interested is when disaster strikes. As a consultant, I usually do not get called in until deep trouble looms.

However, one large oil company asked me to work with its management team. After a single day, I told the chief executive officer. "As well as things are going, I have not figured out what you want me for. It looks as though you have a fairly good management system, and things are going well."

His response typifies the point of this vignette: "We want to do better. We do not want to relax. We think we can raise productivity and manage even better."

This concept shows that management and parenting do have common problems. In both cases, management development and training makes the task easier and the

Part II: Practical Applications of Common Sense Management

"organization" more efficient. Parents need to learn to recognize the various levels of growth in their children and train them in preparation for the next stage. just as good management does those working immediately under them.

Proverbs 22:6 can be directly applied from parenting to management. *The Amplified Bible* especially makes this scripture clear.

> **Train up a child in the way he should go [and in keeping with his individual gift or bent), and when he is old he will not depart from it.**

Each child's business, church, and nonprofit has its own special abilities, gifts, and talents (resources and abilities). These talents (resources) should be utilized to their fullest. But instruction and guidance are required to help the child (business) fully develop. We need the guidance and wisdom from God to help us train (manage) a child (business).

Part II: Practical Applications of Common Sense Management

Stinger Principle

Stinger Principle

The "Stinger Principle" was inspired by bees. If you do not let employees know things are going as they should or are not going as they should, people tend to be uncertain, experience anxiety, and not perform as well. Only after objectives have been set and explained, and it is obvious there has been no real attempt to meet them, should employees (or children)get an appropriate stinger if goals are not met. The well-placed stinger gets the attention. What happens in some organizations is that people get very high ratings or no performance feedback at all, then suddenly are fired or replaced. The organization does not have a candid appraisal system. If a person is off target, he should get a stinger as a signal to get back on target.

In performance appraisal many employers tend to gloss over things, to say, "You are doing just fine, we appreciate your hard work, it is good you showed up for the company picnic, and you did well in our golf tournament," but they never get down to brass tacks about actual performances. What did you agree was to be accomplished, and did he do it? If he did not, you need to apply the stinger: "Here is what was expected on the job. You have not accomplished the key results. You are going to have to adjust your performance."

I believe people want to know how they stand. Only by knowing where they stand can corrections be made, thus assuring a better chance of success. SLRP/MBO, with its regular review, provides the opportunity for praise or the stinger. One of the best analogies to draw from scripture when looking at this principle is the similar relationship of parent and employer with child and employee. Both the

Part II: Practical Applications of Common Sense Management

parent and employer are in positions of authority and are, to a certain extent, responsible for the actions of the child and employee. Proverbs 23:13 tells us to discipline children to save them from death. Proverbs 29:17 says this disciplining will bring you peace, and your child will bring delight to your soul as a result.

Christians know they are to pattern their lives after Jesus, and how many times did He correct people? In John 8:11, he tells the woman caught in adultery to leave her life of sin. In Matthew 16:23, he tells Peter to get out of his sight for not thinking of things of God but things of men. Proverbs 3:12 (NIV) says the Lord disciplines those he loves, so we ought to discipline those we care about.

> **Do not hold back discipline from the child,**
> **Although you beat him with the rod, he will not die.**
>
> **You shall beat him with the rod,**
> **And deliver his soul from Sheol.**
>
>   Proverbs 23:13, 14 NAS
>
> **Correct your son. and he will give you comfort;**
> **He will also delight your soul.**
>
>   Proverbs 29: 17 NAS

Common Sense Management—A Biblical Perspective

Part II: Practical Applications of Common Sense Management

Cycle Theory

Cycle Theory

Some time ago, I began to notice that in athletics, business and organizations, things tend to run in cycles.

When I was in junior high, I remember reading about St. Louis University, Eddie Hickey, and the battle for the Missouri Valley Conference basketball title. In 1954, Oklahoma A&M had Bob Kurland, and Oklahoma City University had Hub Reed. During 1984, St. Louis University and Oklahoma City University were both at an ebb. Who would have believed in 1955 that high-ranking St. Louis University basketball someday would be in such a low spot in its quest for success? But they hit a "down cycle:' Both schools are now on the rebound.

I have noticed the same thing occurs in companies and organizations. In some ways, they tend to go through cycles. If you are aware of this fact, then as you start into a down cycle, you can begin to be aware of management changes.

A set of "flash points" should be set. The specific events that "flash" the downturn should be identified early. Most organizations hit bottom before reacting. The steps of the strategic-planning process can help an organization spot the start of a new cycle and also help it react and pull out rather than go all the way through the full cycle.

Staying alert and monitoring the environment is a scriptural principle. Studying the cycles and behavior of other organizations can help you avoid the same mistakes. The scriptures on the next page reinforce the "cycle theory" and show that God expects His people to manage their affairs

Part II: Practical Applications of Common Sense Management

wisely. Christians should not pray for guidance, and then blindly follow their feelings. Planning and monitoring are an integral part of the Christian walk.

> Let your eyes look right on [with fixed purpose],
> and let your gaze be straight before you.
>
> Consider well the path of your feet, and let all
> your ways be established and ordered aright.
> Proverbs 4:25-26 AMP
>
> Accordingly then, let us not sleep, as the rest do,
> but let us keep wide awake (alert. watchful. cautious
> and on our guard) and let us be sober (calm, collected
> and circumspect).
> I Thessalonians 5:6 AMP
>
> But test and prove all things [until you
> can recognize] what is good; [to that] hold fast.
> 1 Thessalonians 5:21 AMP
>
> Let me warn you therefore, beloved, that knowing
> these things beforehand. you should be on your guard
> lest you be carried away by the error of lawless and
> wicked [persons and] fall from your own [present]
> firm condition-your own steadfastness [of mind].
> 2 Peter 3:17 AMP

Common Sense Management—A Biblical Perspective

Part II: Practical Applications of Common Sense Management

Pay Me Now or Pay Me Later

Pay Me Now or Pay Me Later

The "pay me now, or pay me later" principle means if you do not take time to set up a workable plan with objectives, sooner or later you will have to *take* the time to straighten out your organization. If you do not spend time in the beginning, you will spend time later. There are no shortcuts to good management and planning.

I was reminded of this recently when a representative of an organization in deep trouble came to me pleading, "You have to bail us out; you're the only one who can help." When the company was organized, I was asked to help. I shared the process of strategic planning and what was essential in setting up an organization to run consistently. But the president said, "Take six weeks to set an overall plan and have committees work on the purpose of the organization? We don't have time. We have to get in the marketplace. We'll just hire people and get going;' I have seen the same thing happen time after time. Now this organization has almost reached the point where its survival is doubtful. Its leader is anguished and floundering. The planning process is a must, an insurance policy, for success. You need to slow down and develop a plan to have a reasonable chance to succeed.

Proverbs 24:3 (NIV) says, By wisdom a house is built, and through understanding it is established.

Proverbs 28:16 (NIV) says, A tyrannical ruler lacks judgment, (include employees in decision making).

Part II: Practical Applications of Common Sense Management

Proverbs 22:3 (NIV) says, A prudent man sees danger and takes refuge, but the simple keep going and suffer for it.

Common Sense Management—A Biblical Perspective

Part II: Practical Applications of Common Sense Management

Afraid to Fail

Anyone would walk a 2 x 4 plank on the ground for $100, but raise the plank a hundred feet in the air and there would be few takers. People, by nature, are afraid to take risks, afraid of failing. But you cannot develop to your potential without taking some risks. I know a youngster who dove off the high board at a local pool all summer on frequent trips with his grandfather. One day his well-meaning mother was there, concerned and nervous, warning the child of all potential dangers. His next dive did not go as well, and before long he completely stopped diving. This ability to create a self-fulfilling prophecy contributes to fear of failure.

When you go to war against your enemies and see horses and chariots and an army greater than yours. do not be afraid of them because the Lord your God, who brought you up out of Egypt, will be with you ...(Deut. 20:1 NIV). Men of Israel. Listen, today you are going into a battle. Do not be afraid of your enemies or lose courage or panic!

A self-fulfilling prophecy that gives negative reinforcement stems from failed courage and panic. The Lord says that to be successful, victorious, or prosperous, His people should face circumstances with all possible God-given courage, bravery, and self-confidence. The steps of a good man are ordered by the Lord: and he delighteth in his way (Ps. 37:23). Only God knows the unfinished buildings, campaigns, and other projects that have failed because of naive leaders and/or fearful followers.

Part II: Practical Applications of Common Sense Management

Common Sense Management—A Biblical Perspective

Defensive End Theory

I was a defensive end in my football-playing days In an 8-3 formation with one assignment: to hit the offensive end, and then proceed to knock down everyone one I could. I played three years of varsity football with this idea ingrained in my thinking. As I began to see how organizations operate, I saw that spotting problems means confronting them. When I spot trouble, rather than skirt it, shrug it off, or hope it will go away, I immediately round up the persons involved and go straight to the source with zeal to resolve it. The "defensive end" theory is: if you spot trouble, go after it and solve it.

As I came into new jobs, one of the things I could count on was that the union, in most cases, was there to oppose management. I began to notice that previous managers played the appeasement game, and it did not work. I am not anti-union. Unions exist because management had not met its responsibility over a long period of time. If people are treated fairly, their needs are met, and they have a sense of participation and well-being, they do not need a union. As I began to see that a appeasement fails, my basic routine in a new job was to say, "Here is what we are going to do, here is where we are going, and if you have a problem, let's get it resolved now:' I got the issue out on the table right at the beginning.

> Finally, my brethren, be strong in the Lord, and in the power of his might (Eph. 6:10). The Bible tells us we can take a strong stand. We do have the power to overcome problems. Christians must control problems, not be continually reacting to problems.

Part II: Practical Applications of Common Sense Management

Common Sense Management—A Biblical Perspective

Alamo Theory: Toe the Line

I have been using this philosophy since 1968: "Here is where we are; here is where we are going; here is the management system we are going to *use:*

After outlining the strategic-planning/MBO concept, I say: "If you are with me, here is the line; step across. Now here is how we are going to manage. If you do not believe in this management system. then I will help you find another job in this organization, another job somewhere else. or you will be fired."

I learned that lesson the hard way in a manufacturing assignment with my own management team. The company had planned to close the plant if it did not become productive. Soon I had gotten through to everyone else with "Here is how we are going to do business," and so forth. But I began to notice my whole management team was playing games with me. I was hearing everything I wanted to hear, but I was not seeing enough action - management resists change just as everyone else.

Finally, I called a meeting, let my blood pressure mount as high as I dared, and just had it out.

I said, "Look, I am clearing the decks. You guys will not be here next week if you do not get on the stick. *Here* is *how we are going to manage: here* is *how we are going to do it.* Are you with me?"

Part II: Practical Applications of Common Sense Management

That got their attention, and from then on the story was that of a dramatic turnaround, one which was very profitable and helped resolve a bad situation.

You have to get people cooperating with you, and by meeting problems head-on and explaining to the people involved exactly how you are going to manage, you are in better shape to assure success.

The Bible tells us that we have the right to ask for loyalty and support.

> He who scorns instruction will pay for it, but he who respects a command is rewarded.
> Proverbs 13:13 NIV

> Then Moses stood in the gate of the camp, and said, Who is on the Lord's side? let him come unto me.
> Exodus 32:26

> A servant cannot be corrected by mere words; though he understands, he will not respond.
> Proverbs 29:19 NIV

> He who listens to a life-giving rebuke will be at home among the wise.
> Proverbs 15:31 NIV

> A rebuke impresses a man of discernment more than a hundred lashes a fool.
> Proverbs 17:10 NIV

Common Sense Management—A Biblical Perspective

Part II: Practical Applications of Common Sense Management

Lawn Mowing

Common Sense Management—A Biblical Perspective
Lawn-Mowing Theory

An organization can be compared to a lawn in need of care. The purpose is to get the "lawn" in good shape within a certain time. The management team should look at the total job to be done, and based upon strengths, weaknesses and experience, divide up the work as a crew of workmen would looking at a yard in need of care. Tasks and objectives are set before the work starts. When every one knows the results to be achieved, work begins. Too many organizations work with no plan, no direction, and with people not coordinated. Leadership in these organizations seems to feel there is a noble courage in just letting things work out. In reality, there is a high cost in much waste and confusion. The lawn-mowing theory means looking at the total task, dividing up the work, deciding the best and most economical method, then going to work. People work better when they can tune in on the plan. The Bible tells us we need to work together. Too much disjointed effort is rampant in all organizations today.

> The eye cannot say to the hand, "I don't need you!" And the head cannot say to the feet, "I don't need you!" On the contrary, those parts of the body that seem to be weaker are indispensable.
> **1 Corinthians 12:21, 22** (NIV)

> Behold, how good and how pleasant it is for brethren to dwell together in unity!
> **Psalm 133:1**

Part II: Practical Applications of Common Sense Management

Common Sense Management—A Biblical Perspective

Are You Always Right?

People frequently ask me this. My wife and children rejoice in those instances when things do not turn out as I predict. Tony Andress, a veteran manager with Continental Can Company, helped my wife. Mari (over eight months pregnant with our daughter Theresa at the time), into a chair at a company party in 1966 and said, "Henry has wild ideas, and they always seem to work." I am "really not all that sharp," but I do my homework and study the basics. If 1 see that key people are not being involved in planning a project, it is easy to predict, "This project will not be successful and people will be unhappy in six months. "There is a set of basics that cannot be violated to achieve success. If they are, the results are predictable: failure. A good example is the case of Thomas Edison, the nineteenth century's most successful inventor. Most academic historians agree that he so totally mismanaged the businesses he started that he had to be removed from authority so they could be saved. Books are full of similar stories. Often the person who starts something has trouble managing after it begins to grow. It does not take a genius to spot such a situation and predict trouble. All kinds of things are predictable if we study the basics of strategic planning/MBO and then adjust the plan accordingly.

Part II: Practical Applications of Common Sense Management

Subway

Subway

Once something is started, such as a new product or a new service offered by a business, it becomes like a New York subway -you can't get off when you want to. My sister, Mary Helen, and I discovered this fact of life when we missed a stop and headed on toward Brooklyn.

If you do not check the route along which you (your plan) is traveling, you do not even know where you are going (the destination).

The point is to do a good job of planning and to know in advance where you can get off if things do not go as expected. Some people get on for the ride, do not know where they are going, and do not know how to get off.

The "get-off" plan is *as important as the "get-on" plan.* A contingency plan is needed, along with asking a large number of "what if" questions anytime something is started, or before getting on for the "ride."

Part II: Practical Applications of Common Sense Management

View world with colored Classes

View the World Through (Other) Colored Glasses

I remember the first time I field-dressed a deer on a hunting trip with a surgeon and a dentist as hunting companions. Since I am a results-oriented person, I just concentrated on finishing the job. Both of my companions were in a state of shock as I plodded through the chore. Their field of competence dictated precise cuts and careful cleaning. *Different professions put a high value on different things.* We want others to see things in the same priority of importance as we do. A pastor sees the spiritual base, a businessman looks for results-oriented behavior, and a dentist is interested in oral hygiene. We tend to see the world from the perspective of our own discipline. If a person's orientation is not like yours, you can count on a different view -and misunderstanding, if one does not take the time to learn other viewpoints. The Bible encourages us to be understanding of other people's perspectives.

> And if I have the gift of prophecy, and know all mysteries and all knowledge; and if I have all faith, so as to remove mountains, but do not have love, I am nothing.
> 1 Corinthians 13:2 NAS

> But now God has placed the members, each one of them, in the body, just as He desired.
>
> And if they were all one member, where would the body be?
> 1 Corinthians 12:18 NAS

Part II: Practical Applications of Common Sense Management

Stew in Your own Juice

Common Sense Management—A Biblical Perspective
Stew In Your Own Juice

If people are not involved in the planning, it is your plan - not theirs. People will not "buy into" anything unless they have input. Whoever executes the plan must be involved in the plan. My strategic planning steps force this interaction. If you do not get everyone involved, your subordinates will let you "stew in your own juice." Organization veterans have perfected this strategy. The general feeling is to go along with as little effort and support as possible.

> But I did not want to do anything without your consent, so that any favor you do will be spontaneous and not forced.
> **Philemon 14 NIV**

> ... he which soweth sparingly shall reap also sparingly.
> **2 Corinthians 9:6a**

> Be not deceived! God is not mocked: for whatsoever a man soweth, that shall he also reap.
> **Galatians 6:7**

A manager is sowing good seeds when he his people in plans that affect them. The harvest will be loyalty and support for the plan.

Part II: Practical Applications of Common Sense Management

Snowball

Snowball

Get some positive motion going, even if you must give it a push. At Continental Can Company Stock-yards, the press manufacturing area had run in the red for five years before mid-October 1967 when I instituted SLRP/MBO, training programs, new preventive-maintenance programs, and so forth.

That was the same year New York Jets quarterback Joe Namath said, "We will beat the Colts in the Super Bowl."

People gave the press department at CCC about as much chance of running in the black as the Jets winning the Super Bowl. A theme was developed, however, that we *could* do it. After implementing Strategic Planning/MBO, we finally ran in the black. Once we did it, the "snowball effect" hit, and we were off and running with ten straight weeks of topnotch performance.

Another example is Roger Bannister's four-minute mile in 1954. Once the barrier was broken, others achieved the same result.

In certain situations, a manager is trying to create momentum out of a lifeless mess. But once started in motion, snowballs and organizations seem to move on their own momentum.

> **Now finish the work, so that your eager willingness to do it may be matched by your completion of it, according to your means.**
> **2 Corinthians 8:11 NIV**

Part II: Practical Applications of Common Sense Management

Get Your Head Above the Clouds

Common Sense Management—A Biblical Perspective
Get Your Head Above the Clouds

Do not just work from day-to-day. Do not let the daily pressures dictate your actions. Get control by looking ahead. Get your head above the clouds and see where you are going. An airline pilot has radar in his plane and help from airport tower operators to give him instructions in getting through the clouds. If he does not, he can become disoriented and even confused as to which way is up or down. An organization must get above the clouds and look out to the horizon to see where it is going. Some individuals go through their entire life-spans going now here, having no direction. Also, this is the way many organizations are run -no direction, lost in the clouds. Strategic planning forces you to look toward the future, which gives organization and structure to the day-to-day tasks and decisions.

Two Scripture verses that address this topic are in Proverbs: *In all thy ways acknowledge him, and he shall direct thy paths (Prov. 3:6)*, and *A man's heart deviseth his way: but the lord directeth his steps (Prov. 16:9)*. Those two verses seem to contradict serious long-term planning. They seem to say "Be faithful and the Lord will tell you what to do." But my interpretation is to plan-fast-think-pray for direction. We use the best of man's methods, and then our spirit confirms God's will.

Part II: Practical Applications of Common Sense Management

Homeostasis

Homeostasis is a theory from the science of biology. One definition is: A relatively stable state of equilibrium, or a tendency toward such a state, between the different but interdependent elements of -or groups of elements of an organism or group.

This theory suggests that a firm reacts to the outside environment as well as factors inside the organization and drifts toward a stable state of equilibrium. If this tendency does, in fact, affect organizations, management must recognize its responsibility to see that the equilibrium reached is a positive, productive one. Sometimes I wonder what effect management really has on organizations overtime. Management appears at time to just be along for the ride. It takes effort and a sense of conviction to force an organization to follow a positive track. You could also call this the lither most at or thermometer theory:' A thermostat reads the temperature conditions or environment and adjusts the heater or air conditioner to meet the desired goal. A thermometer goes up and down with the environment. About the Tower of Babel, God said:

> If as one people speaking the same language they have begun to do this, then them nothing they plan to do will be impossible for (Gen. 11:6 **NIV**). Romans 12:2 (**NIV**) says, Do not conform any longer to the pattern **of** this world, but be transformed **by** the renewing of your mind. Then you will be able to test and approve what God's will is his good, pleasing and perfect will.

Part II: Practical Applications of Common Sense Management

Seed Faith

Borrowed from Oral Roberts, former president of ORU, this Biblical theory is derived from Jesus' teachings on seed planting and harvests. (Matt. 7:17-20, 12:34b-35.)

As a farmer uses his best corn to plant the crop and expects a good harvest, so a person is to plant good seeds of deeds, love, friendship, and money and expect to receive a great harvest from the Lord.

A firm plants seeds of service to the community and expects to receive a harvest of goodwill. A good employer pays taxes, makes a profit to ensure his firm's long-term survival, provides a good product or service, acts in an ethical manner and keeps the welfare of his employees and the community in mind. These good seeds planted will result in good labor-management relations, as well as harvests of profits and a fair rate of return for investors.

Each time I have planted a seed of time, money, or prayer, it has returned as a harvest. I am thankful to Oral Roberts for helping me learn this principle.

See my web site www.hmigliore.com. A link coveys a visit with Oral Roberts a few months before he passed.

> Give, and it shall be given unto you; good measure, pressed down, and shaken together, and running over, shall men give into your bosom. For with the same measure that ye mete withal it shall be measured to you again.
>
> **Luke 6:38**

Part II: Practical Applications of Common Sense Management

Natural Rhythm

Natural Rhythm

There is a natural rhythm to life. The tides, moon, and sun function on a natural cycle. There is a natural rhythm to living. Interacting with society and with our loved ones, growth in our spiritual lives, and good health -all these factors must be in rhythm for a person to be successful.

Throughout my career, I have been associated with many "turnaround" experiences in which poorly performing organizations have gotten their acts together and become successful. The first was Continental Can's No. 73 in St. Louis. That experience is documented in my book. MBG: Blue Collar to Top Executive. The latest has been Liberty Industries in Ohio. The methods in my books and articles seem to generate a natural rhythm. There is a rhythm to success. Although I find it hard to describe, there seems to be a "motion" that must be initiated for an organization to prosper. The combination of beginning meetings, communication, and looking ahead all seem to get the motion started. Then a natural success rhythm begins -success is just around the corner.

From several passages of Scripture, it is clear that this natural rhythm comes from the will of the Lord so that it behooves us to find out His will and get in tune with it.

> **Except the Lord build the house, they labour in vain that build it.**
> **Psalm 127:1a**

> **This book of the law shall not depart from your mouth, but you shall meditate on it day and night. so that you may be careful to do according to all that is written in it: for then you will make your way prosperous, and then you will have success.**

Part II: Practical Applications of Common Sense Management

Joshua 1:8 NAS

To everything there is a season, and a time to every purpose under the heaven:

A time to be born. and a time to die; a time to plant. and a time to pluck up that which is planted;

A time to kill, and a time to heal; a time to breakdown, and a time to build up;

A time to weep, and a time to laugh; a time to mourn, and a time to dance;

A time to cast away stones. and a time to gather stones together; a time to embrace, and a time to refrain from embracing;

A time to get. and a time to lose; a time to keep, and a time to cast away;

A time to rend. and a time to sew; a time to keep silence, and a time to speak;

A time to love, and a time to hate; a time of war, and a time of peace.

Ecclesiastes 3:1-8

Common Sense Management—A Biblical Perspective

Part II: Practical Applications of Common Sense Management

Common Sense Management—A Biblical Perspective

"I'll Be True to You While You're Gone, Honey Just Don't Be Gone Too Long"

This theme of a country-western song is the basis for good public relations. Identify the important people who impact your organization and be sure you personally interact with them on a regular basis. The interaction can be social, luncheon meetings, guest speaking, company picnics, and so forth. If you do not give them the personal touch, someone else will. Too often, we seek someone only when there are problems. A relationship must be well established before trouble hits.

I have followed this practice for years. I meet with, correspond, and talk with all the people who are important to me. For example, Bobby Parker, chairman of Parker Drilling in Tulsa, has supported my work for years. Recently when the third edition of Strategic Long- Range Planning came out, I autographed a copy and hand-delivered it to him. I said, "Thanks Mr. Parker" and we chatted a few minutes. I could have mailed it to him and saved myself a lot of time. But I appreciate him as a person and wanted him to know it.

Be hospitable to one another without complaint.

As each one has received a special gift, employ it in serving one another, as good stewards of the manifold grace of God.

                                        1 Peter 4:9,10 NAS

Part II: Practical Applications of Common Sense Management

Common Sense Management—A Biblical Perspective

Get Out of the Ghetto

Analyze your strengths and strengthen your weaknesses. Find out what you do best and capitalize on it. If you do not like your station in life, go to work. Do not wait for a break -make the break happen. I have known many people who talk a good game and do nothing. Use your energy to make and carry out a plan, not to sit and complain about the situation. A significant amount of energy in America goes into complaining and criticizing, not into changing the situation. After you do your best, you can ask God for His best. Many minority Americans use athletics to "get out of the ghetto:' We all must find a way out of some sort of ghetto. As the three men in Matthew 25, we should take the talents God gives us and use them to the best of our abilities. Three slaves were given talents (money): the first, five; the second. two; and the third, one, each according to his ability. The first two immediately began to work toward their desired results. They doubled what was given them and proved worthy to be placed in charge of many things. The third was afraid to try anything. He buried his talent, so it was taken from him and given to someone else.

Some are given more talent than others, but each has been given some. One unique aspect of America is that each person has an opportunity to progress, if he desires to do so. We should be good stewards of our talents by developing them to their limits for the glory of the Lord. Through hard work and the opportunity God provides, one can find a way "out of the ghetto:'

Part II: Practical Applications of Common Sense Management

Common Sense Management—A Biblical Perspective

Find Out He Is a Christian by How He Acts, Not by What He Says

I have found that when a company or person uses a "Christian" orientation as a sales pitch, you can expect \ trouble is on the way. I would rather learn they are Christians by the way they do business and then have them tell me as a confirmation of what I already know. I have lectured on this point many times, often asking for a show of hands in the audience of those that have had the same experience. When I ask for those who have lost out on a business deal or transaction when the person or business made a point of stressing the Christian dimension in the early part of the discussion, hands always go up.

> Let your light so shine before men, that they may see your good works, and glorify your Father which is in heaven.
>
> Matthew 5:16

> Yea. a man may say, Thou hast faith, and I have works: shew me thy faith without thy works, and I will shew thee my faith by my works.
>
> James 2:18

> Having your conversation honest among the Gentiles: that, whereas they speak against you as evildoers, they may by your good works, which they shall behold, glorify God in the day of visitation.
>
> 1 Peter 2:12

Part II: Practical Applications of Common Sense Management

Be the Best You Can Be

Common Sense Management—A Biblical Perspective
Be the Best You Can Be

We spend too much time comparing ourselves With others. Class reunions turn out to be a time for comparison. Do not worry about other people. Be concerned with your progress. Be the best you can be. Set realistic goals and compare your performance as you attempt to meet them. God gave all of us skills and missions. Those with more talents have responsibilities to use them positively.

The following scriptures support this:

> And whatever you do in word or deed, do all in the name of the Lord Jesus, giving thanks through Him to God the Father (Col. 3:17 NAS). Finally then, brethren, we request and exhort you in the Lord Jesus, that, as you received from us instruction as to how you ought to walk and please God (just as you actually do walk), that you may excel still more (1 Thess. 4:1 NAS). Do you not know that those who run in a race all run, but only one receives the prize? Run in such a way that you may win (1 Cor. 9:24 NAS).
>
> Colossians 3:17 shows us all we do should be done In the most excellent way possible. Anything less is not a suitable offering to the Lord. First Thessalonians 4:1 makes it clear that it is God's desire to see us excel in all we do. First Corinthians 9:24 is an encouragement to Christians to settle for nothing less than being a winner. This passage even seems to encourage a competitive attitude. It seems very clear God expects our best in all we do. If further evidence were needed, Luke 19:12-27 reinforces the idea of developing our talents to the fullest potential. Anything less is not acceptable.

Part II: Practical Applications of Common Sense Management

Common Sense Management—A Biblical Perspective

Never Give Up

When I played basketball in high school for the Collinsville Cardinals, we were behind seven points playing at Jenks with 19 seconds left. Somehow we tied the game and won. I will admit there was an element of luck, but we were pressing and playing all out to win. If we had given up, we would have lost. You are never beaten as long as you are trying to win.

God wants all His people to do their best in everything that they do, as the Bible states in 1 Corinthians 9:24 NAS: Do you not know that those who a run in a race all run, but only one receives the prize? Run in such a way that you may win.

Doing your best means not giving up when times get tough, but rather putting your trust in the lord and continuing to try. The Bible is the best example of this, It is really hard to choose a few particular verses that exemplify this, but rather it is easier to choose a few prime examples, such as Moses, Job, and Jesus. Moses was a man of great knowledge and power during his time as the Pharaoh's son. After being exiled out of Egypt, Moses met the lord and was given his task. Against the odds, he went to do the work of the lord. During this time, Moses met with many trials and failures as he was freeing the Israelites from bondage, but he never once gave up and walked away. He put his faith in God and accomplished his task.

Part II: Practical Applications of Common Sense Management

Do It When It's Important

Common Sense Management—A Biblical Perspective
Do It When It Is Important

Flowers before and after an anniversary make this point. After twenty years of marriage, if the flowers are there April 4, our anniversary is special. The timing is right. If they are presented in May, the opportunity is lost. If a person working for you does a good job or does something special tell him right then, not later or not at all.

> **Withhold not good from them to whom it is due, when it is in the power of thine hand to do it.**
>
> **Say not unto thy neighbour, Go, and come again, and tomorrow I will give; when thou hast it by thee.**
>
> Proverbs 3:27,28

Part II: Practical Applications of Common Sense Management

Success—the Whole Person

Success in life is based upon developing your own strengths to become what the Lord wants you to be. Success in all areas is what is important; spiritual, family, profession, health and contribution to your fellow man. Too often we define success in terms of our career and financial goals. Set goals in other areas: vacations with family, helping others, reading books, and so forth. Be successful in all you do. I have known many successful career people whose personal lives are in shambles. Work had become almost a refuge to get away from their families. Although it is not true in all cases, when I see someone on the job and working all hours, I suspect lack of fulfillment in other areas of life.

> **Dear friend, I pray that you may enjoy good health and that all may go well with you, even as your soul is getting along well.**
> 3 John 2 NIV

> **Do not wear yourself out to get rich; have the wisdom to show restraint.**
> Proverbs 23:4 NIV

Part II: Practical Applications of Common Sense Management

Be There in the Morning

Be There in the Morning

This theory—which emphasizes loyalty—is a key factor to success. It is based on dependability and trust. I have seen promotions go to less-qualified persons based on this key factor. Trust is important! I do not want anyone working for me who I do not feel is loyal to our mission and to me. Dr. Eugene Jennings of Michigan State, after a lifetime of work studying careers, has reached this same general conclusion. Loyalty is not something you can teach or perhaps learn. But be aware of this factor so you can better understand organization life.

> **Most men will proclaim every one his own goodness: but a faithful man who can find?**
> **Proverbs 20:6**

> **Who then is a faithful and wise servant, whom his lord hath made ruler over his household, to give them meat in due season?**
>
> **Blessed is that servant, whom his lord when he cometh shall find so doing.**
> **Matthew 24:45, 46**

Part II: Practical Applications of Common Sense Management

We All Get In Trouble when We Get Too Fat

Excess Weight Breeds Trouble

This theory applies to the human body as well as organizations. Overstaffing an organization is like being overweight—it slows you down.

I notice that when my weight gets over two hundred and thirty pounds, my blood pressure goes up. I tire easily and do not have as much vigor.

The same thing happens with organizations. Good objective-setting with a hard look at results keeps an organization lean. Every resource must contribute to achieving key results.

Part II: Practical Applications of Common Sense Management

Keep It Simple

We tend to make things too complicated. A few basics are keys to success in any endeavor. Lee Iacocca says the keys to managing the Chrysler Corporation are the letter of commitment and the quarterly review. Vince Lombardi, the legendary coach of the Green Bay Packers, lists three things that lead to success:

1. You have to start by teaching the fundamentals. A player has to know the basics of the game and how to play his position.

2. You have to keep the player in line. That is discipline. The men have to play as a team, not as a bunch of individuals. There is no room for prima donnas.

3. You have got to care for one another. You have to love one another. Each player has to be thinking about the next guy. The difference between mediocrity and greatness is the feeling these players have for one another. Most people call it "team spirit." When the players are imbued with that special feeling, you know you have yourself a winning team.

If a few basic fundamentals are covered in any endeavor, it is likely to be successful. First Corinthians 1:27, 28 says God chose the weak, lowly, despised things to shame the wise and strong. Romans 12:9 says love must be sincere. Be devoted to one another.

Part II: Practical Applications of Common Sense Management

Common Sense Management—A Biblical Perspective

Pine Tree

After many hunting and fishing trips in the North Country, I began to reflect on the life cycle of pine trees. Many with a weak root system grow tall but topple by the weight of their own growth. People and organizations do the same thing. Without a solid foundation, success and momentum cause their demise. The solid foundation for an organization is dedication, belief in free enterprise, and a well-thought-out plan. I have seen people and organizations "hit it lucky" on timing in a market, product mix, or just by being in the right place at the right time, then become convinced success was based on their insight and direction. However, they never learn to plan or manage. Sooner or later, success creates a monster they cannot manage, and boom they fail. First Peter 2 talks about maturing in God's wisdom. Growth in Christ does not come all at once; it is a lifetime process. We are strengthened every day we seek Him. We will not fall, unless we disobey. Organizations and people are healthier and sturdier, just as pine trees, if the growth process is gradual. They are likelier to stand for a longer period of time. Matthew 7 ends with a parable, a straightforward and bold story: Those who build their lives on the Word will find security and stability, those who do not will come to ruin. Laying this foundation takes time and there are no shortcuts. Organizations must also build their existences on stable ground. This is accomplished by setting a short-and long-range plan and following it. Otherwise, the entity can become unmanageable, unstable, and vulnerable to disaster.

Part II: Practical Applications of Common Sense Management

Common Sense Management—A Biblical Perspective

Failing to Prepare Is Like Preparing to Fail

The keys to sports success are preparation and practice. My coaches always said, "You will play like you practice."

I still remember the first pass I caught against Tulsa Central in a 1958 football game. Our quarterback and my lifelong friend, Clay Lynch, and I had practiced our pass patterns for years. One summer we went to the city park in Collinsville every night and ran this pattern. So it was no accident that we connected on three straight passes in that game. We had practiced, and we believed in each other. Thoroughly plan and prepare, and you are more likely to succeed. Without planning and preparation, you guarantee failure. I would rather over-prepare with full planning and input from everyone than make a fast decision based on few facts and emotion. Often you save time in the short run, only to find time is lost owing to costly mistakes in the long run. Proper planning is like buying insurance for success. There are always those little things that must be considered that affect the success of the venture.

For lack of guidance a nation falls, but many advisers make victory sure.
Proverbs 11:14 NIV

Part II: Practical Applications of Common Sense Management

The Product Must Be Better Than the Sales Pitch

The late Oral Roberts once used the phrase, "The product must be better than the sales pitch:' as part of a talk to a group of marketing managers attending an ORU School of Business seminar. He drew the analogy between the product he was selling-Jesus and the Christian walk -and business.

Marketing managers must believe in their products in the same way, with an underlying theme of honesty and integrity. The product or service must really help people and organizations meet their needs. When you believe in what you are selling, you can get excited. Too many times, the emphasis is on the sales pitch -get it sold and do not worry about the customer or consumer. A gaudy sales pitch creates expectations which, if not met by the product, create a dissatisfied customer -one who will not return!

Part II: Practical Applications of Common Sense Management

The O-Ring

Common Sense Management—A Biblical Perspective

The O-Ring

Lee Iacocca said it, and it continues to be painfully true: Success confirms what we already know, and the only way we learn is from failure.[1] It is unfortunate that we are aroused only by gigantic failure and tragedy. We all learned from the Nixon resignation that if you make a mistake, you should admit it in a hurry. I am calling this the "fess up" theory. If you have done a good job as a leader, your subordinates are going to understand and allow for a few mistakes. Like everyone else, make my share. What I am continuing to learn to do is just say, "Well, I blew it on that one." make the proper apologies if needed, and "keep right on trucking."

Now we have the great tragedy of the shuttle disaster. What the task force found was a colossal failure of the management system. Fortune Magazine discussed the National Aeronautics and Space Administration (NASA} saying:[2]

"Top executives cannot afford to be isolated from the people below, who are in better touch with what is going on, and cannot afford to set unrealistic goals."

Yet not even this conclusion goes to the heart of the trouble at NASA. The flaw—call it an institutional virtue gone wrong—can trip many companies with overweening ambitions. In its widely hailed report on the tragedy, the commission headed by former Secretary of State William P. Rogers

---

[1] Iacocca. Lee. Iacocca: An Autobiography (New York: Bantam Books. 1984).
[2] Burck. Charles E. Fortune July 7, 1986. P. 8.

Part II: Practical Applications of Common Sense Management
criticized "NASAis legendary 'can do' attitude." The agency, Rogers and his colleagues admonished, cannot do everything.

Senator John Glenn went further. The can-do spirit, he noted, worked perfectly well in the old days, when it included a powerful commitment to safety. In Glenn's view, "can do" gave way over the years to "an arrogant 'cannot fail' attitude:' Managements assumed that no matter what risks they took, the shuttle would succeed.

There must be a system of checks and balances, and a way to listen to the organization. I still remember an incident early in my career when I learned this lesson by accident, and luckily, did not need a big failure to learn it. I was responsible for the industrial engineering function at the time. Working with the research and development staff members and corporate engineers, we redesigned a system to handle the flow of liquids in the plant. It was an engineering marvel, and it was sure to bring me, at age 27, a fair amount of credibility when it worked properly and saved the company hundreds of thousands of dollars. The night before the big "launch," when we would go over to the new system, I came back into the plant and was nervously pacing the floor, looking things over.

As I walked down one of the production lines, a night shift electrician walked by and sort of growled, "It'll never work."

"What does that old goose know?" I thought, "Somebody ought to check his work record."

I continued to walk, but I began to get an uneasy feeling. I turned around, and since I did not know his name, just hollered, "Hey, just a second."

Common Sense Management—A Biblical Perspective

I was not ready to admit he knew something that I did not. After all, I had some talented people working for me. But I asked him why it would not work. He gave me a simple, direct, sixty-second answer. I asked him why he had not said something months before, and his reply was:

"I quit making suggestions years ago when I noticed no one paid any attention. I could have saved this company thousands of dollars, but a person just tires of no one paying any attention."

He then walked off into the shadows of the plant, and I called my boss at home that night, incredibly embarrassed, but insistent that the startup on the new system could not go the next day and explained why. The next morning, I assembled my staff and explained what the old electrician had shared with me. The room was quiet, and then all of them agreed, "He is right."

We quickly redesigned a different component for the system, and even though the startup was delayed, it was successful. I really learned a lesson on that one. At the time, at least I thought I had, and it paid off again years later when I held a key manufacturing position. The layout people had come up with a complete redesign of the manufacturing layout for the entire plant. They had been working on the project for months and had brought in outside architects, consultants, and others. However, when they made their final presentation, something clicked in my mind.

I had approved it, my management team had approved it, but something said, "You had better ask people."

Part II: Practical Applications of Common Sense Management

I told the lead presenter that if he would make the same presentation to a select group of maintenance people - electricians, truck drivers, and workers on the production line - and they approved it, then I would finally sign my approval. A number of people in the room laughed, and that only made me more determined.

I said, "No presentation, no signature." and that started some intellectual fisticuffs that nearly got out of hand. But we set up the presentation for the next day, and guess what? A thirty-year grandmother-type worker, who had come into the plant to man the production line during World War II and stayed on through all the years, had a strange look on her face. Everybody else was talking, but I could tell she wanted to say something.

I shut up the rest of the room and asked her what she thought. She was so nervous that she spoke hesitantly and had a little trouble getting started. Then she shared that the production line on which she worked had been modified in the early 1950s, along the lines of the new design and that the spoilage and downtime rates increased dramatically. She had worked on that line as a young woman and had all kinds of difficulty keeping it open. The engineers and layout people said that just could not be right and "get on with the show."

By then, my heels were dug in, and I was ready for the fight. After we excused the people assembled, we had it out the rest of the afternoon. I told them I would not sign the final authorization until a study was done to see if she was right. Sure enough, she was 100 percent right, and the entire project was scrapped. I will never forget her coming by my office and meekly apologizing for stirring up trouble. I thanked her,

Common Sense Management—A Biblical Perspective

assured her that I enjoyed conflict and that she had done a great job and saved us a fortune.

This incident occurred in February 1968. Since then I have never consciously made a move of any importance without asking advice, approval and recommendations from everyone around me, including the people who are doing the work. Even the Bible tells us to ask for advice.

> **For lack of guidance a nation falls, but many advisers make victory sure.**
> **Proverbs 11:14 NIV**

> **Plans fail for lack of counsel, but with many advisers they succeed.**
> **Proverbs 15:22 NIV**

> **Listen to advice and accept instruction, and in the end you will be wise.**
> **Proverbs 19:20 NIV**

As I work with organizations throughout America, I am amazed to find many management groups violating this principle. All you have to do is look at the unfinished highways, botched computer systems, and empty stores, and wonder how many of these failures could be traced primarily to the very principles we are discussing. If America truly wants to compete on an international basis, we must quit giving lip service to how we use our most valuable resource people. In spite of everything that is being written and said, the way we value, plan, and manage our most important resource in many cases is all talk and no action. Our economic future, and possibly the preservation of the society in which we live, is going to be based on how we use our human resources.

Part II: Practical Applications of Common Sense Management

I am hoping that it does not take a tragic failure for Americans to learn each of the very simple principles of management. Equally important is controlling the arrogance that creeps into the executive suite. One thing the 1980s have taught us is that we can fail -and there is plenty of evidence around us to prove it.

How You Use Today Determines How Tomorrow Uses You

Make the most of each day you live
Do not take anything for granted.
Be a good steward of the gifts God has given you.
Invest your time instead of spending it.
Along with challenges come new opportunities.

Be Content With What You Have and Not With What You Are

Be satisfied with your possessions and belongings.

Do not let greed or jealousy creep in. However, always strive to improve the qualities that will make you a better human being and a mere pleasant person to be around - courtesy, honesty, good-naturedness.

Three Kinds of People

People who MAKE things happen.
People who WATCH things happen.
People who WONDER, "What happened?"

I believe God needs us to make things happen. That does not mean we do not pray, trust, and believe, because we do.

It does mean we do our best and then ask God for His best.

Part II: Practical Applications of Common Sense Management

You Win the Race with Heart

Kentucky Derby: The horse runs out of oxygen after the first half mile, then wins on heart. We all have talent, but the Christian should always have heart.

Anger Is Just One Letter Away From Danger

When you are angry, you are not as capable of making good decisions. Anything you say will likely come out wrong. Once something is said, you cannot take it back. If you do not know what you are talking about, keep your mouth shut.

The Best Kind of Pride Compels You to Do Your Very Best Work, Even if No One Is Watching

The right kind of pride is a beautiful characteristic of human nature. It makes us feel good about ourselves. Every job you do is a reflection of yourself. The quality of your work speaks for you.

Faith Sees Where Sight Is Blind

This principle relates to the long-range strategic plan. If there is a true vision for the future of an organization that has a spiritual base, it takes faith to stay on the operating plan. Oral Roberts continues with faith in his pursuit of the vision God has given him even when it defies short-term analysis.

Common Sense Management—A Biblical Perspective

Seven Days without Prayer Makes One Weak

I cannot imagine not praying off and on throughout every day, Dr. Larry Lea, ORU's vice president for spiritual affairs, has developed a way to use the Lord's Prayer as a daily prayer outline.[3] Briefly, the outline goes like this:

Line 1: Our Father which art in Heaven, hallowed be thy name. Hallow means "to praise." Praise God for Who He is in our lives.

Line 2: Thy kingdom come. **Thy will be done in earth, as it is in heaven.** As Christians, we know that God has a will -or a plan- for this world and for each one of our lives.

Line 3: Give us this day our daily bread. Some people believe this line must have gotten in the Lord's Prayer by accident. But I believe that Jesus always said what He meant and meant what He said. He wants us to tell Him what we need and to be specific about it.

Line 4: And forgive us our debts, as we forgive our debtors. If we want God's forgiveness, we must forgive those who hurt us.

Line 5: And lead us not into temptation, but deliver us from evil. How do we .do that? By putting on the whole

---

[3] Dr. Larry lea, Church on the Rock, Rockwall, Texas. Can You Not Tarry One Hour? (Florida: Altamonte Springs, Creation House, 1985).

armor of God in every day in the way Paul described in Ephesians 6:10-17 - just another way of saying that we need to put on the Lord Jesus.

Line 6: For thine is the kingdom, and the power, and the glory, forever. Amen. This line helps us close prayer by praising God.

Unguided Missiles: Some without Warheads

I see many people zipping off here and there, always in a hurry, never accomplishing anything like a missile with no course. When they land, nothing happens. We need a target, and when we hit it, something must happen.

If You Are Average, You Are as Close to the Bottom as to the Top

Most people want to stay in the middle of the pack. They might "talk a good game" but never put anything into their lives to move from average to excellent. God needs us to move to the top.

The Only Place Success Comes Before Work Is in the Dictionary

There are no shortcuts to success. If you think you are going to be successful without good, old-fashioned, hard work, you are only fooling yourself. Many people say to me, "Henry, you are so successful . . . things come so easy for you:' That is not so. I have worked hard all my life. My athletic career as a high school senior is one example. I had a wonderful year, lettered in four sports and made all-conference in football and basketball. Then I was fortunate enough to play football and basketball at Eastern State University.) What people did not see were the years of running and catching passes after work with my friend, quarterback Clay Lynch. I stayed after practice in basketball every day to shoot more baskets. (The janitor at Collinsville High School allowed me in the gym on weekends.) The work paid off. Anything I ever accomplished followed this same pattern.

The Indispensable Man

Sometime when you're feeling important,
Sometime when your ego's in bloom,
Sometime when you take it for granted,
You're the best qualified in the room,

Sometime when you feel that your going,
Would leave an unfillable hole,
Just follow this simple instruction,
And see how it humbles your soul.

Take a bucket and fill it with water,
Put your hand in it up to the wrist.
Pull it out, and the hole that's remaining,
Is a measure of how you'll be missed.

You may splash all you please when

Part II: Practical Applications of Common Sense Management

You enter, You can stir up the water galore,
But stop, and you'll find in a minute
That it looks quite the same as before.

The moral in this quaint example
Is to do just the best that you can.
Be proud of yourself but remember –

THERE'S NO INDISPENSABLE MAN!

From the Lowest Depth There Is a Path to the Loftiest Height

There is a solution to every problem and every situation. The key is to keep praying and be faithful, and God will help find a way.

A LITTLE FELLOW FOLLOWS ME,
I DARE NOT GO ASTRAY.
FOR WHICH DIRECTION I SHALL TAKE,
HE WILL GO THE SELF-SAME WAY.

In many ways the Fellowship of Christian Athletes follows this motto. The example set by athletes is followed by others. We all have the obligation to set a good example.

Clouds That Never Rain

Long-time friend, ORU faculty member, and fisherman Charles (Chuck) Farah, shared this with me: Many people are like clouds that drift in the sky but never really produce rain.

Common Sense Management—A Biblical Perspective
God needs us to "rain." to be productive, to be a positive force for Him.

Key Man

At the Indianapolis 500 there is always a big crowd and lots of excitement with the focus of attention on the drivers. However, as I watched the race one year, I noticed that the man who periodically fills a race car with gas also is a key person.

My Pal, R. G. Voight

A great friend over the years, with whom I share a common birthday, said:

> "All things work together for good, but any one thing by itself may not be good. For example, take a chocolate cake. The only ingredient in it that is good by itself is milk. Who would want to eat the flour, yeast, salt, raw eggs, bitter chocolate, or even the sugar? But put them all together, and they make a delicious cake."

Final Mark of Success Is Humility and How You Are Remembered

The Mary Gladys Migliore Circle was formed in my home church, the Collinsville First United Methodist Church, after my mother passed away in 1972. She was a warm, loving, steady person. She was in many ways like the biblical Andrew, a servant to all around her. Her memory lingers in so many hearts and triggers a question all of us should ask ourselves:

Part II: Practical Applications of Common Sense Management

"How will I be remembered?" I hope I can measure up to my wonderful mother.

Fess Up

Ever wonder what would have happened if former President Richard Nixon had quickly recognized the error of the events that led up to the Watergate scandal and immediately apologized to the country for his own actions and those of his cohorts? When I make a mistake, I admit it quickly.

Teamwork

Jesus Christ fulfilled his mission on earth in three years. In those three years He poured Himself into training twelve men. Those men followed his example and revolutionized the world. How much time do managers put into training, teamwork, and development?

Learn From the Mistakes of Others— You Cannot Live Long Enough to Make Them All Yourself

I am continually amazed at how we all fail to learn from experiences. In the past two thousand years every conceivable mistake has been made, yet mankind continues making the same ones over and over. A case in point as it relates to business: the use of a matrix organization structure in a large hospital.

Once, I attended a professional meeting with a dinner speaker who was a hospital administrator, and in his talk said, "We will be using the matrix structure to get better results."

My heart just sank. The matrix concept can work, but it is very complex, perhaps like flying a 747. Here was a growing Piper Cub organization trying to fly a 747 . . . doomed to failure. It was none of my business, but I met with the man later in his office and pleaded with him to be careful. As I predicted, it did not work and caused havoc because of lack of understanding, confusion, unclear responsibility, and so forth. I would call it a million dollar mistake!

Do Not Learn the Tricks of the Trade Before You Learn the Trade

I learned this when I looked into the possibility of investing in real estate. Tim Myllykangas, whom I got to know at the 1985 Orange Bowl, is doing well in this business. His success is mentioned in the book Nothing Down. He learned the "tricks of the trade" after he invested time and money learning the trade. You should not get into anything without taking time to learn the trade.

Nobody Knows What He Can Do Until He Tries

Former Tulsa Mayor Dick Crawford, and good friend felt he could be of service to the people and community of Tulsa, so he ran for mayor in the 1985 election. Many people said his experience was limited, but he won the election and took a shot at the job he did an outstanding job during the difficult economic times facing the city as well as the state of Oklahoma. He had the courage to try, and it paid off

Noah Did Not Wait for His Ship to Come In—He Built One

Too many Christians are sitting on their hands waiting for God to act. We need to go into action. If we do our best, then we can ask God for His best. Naturally, we pray every step of the way, but the key is to do whatever your hand finds to do.

If you think you are good, then why not be better?

If you think you are better, then be the best.

The Difference Between Good and Great Is a Little Extra Effort

In this competitive world many organizations, churches and people are good at what they do. It is the extra effort that helps achieve a higher level of excellence.

The Surest Way Not to Fail Is to Determine to Succeed

When Oral Roberts announced the building of the City of Faith Medical and Research Center, I began to think about how that would affect the School of Business. At that time, I was dean. Immediately, I visualized people with MBA training helping manage the City of Faith complex. We developed a program to train students for a career in health care. I did not have training in the field, but I felt deep in my spirit that it was the thing to do and was determined the venture would s succeed. Two health care professionals agreed to teach the first course in the fall. In midsummer, they informed me that previous commitments would keep them from teaching. In the next few weeks, two more qualified people accept the job, and then for one reason or another could not teach. By then, school was starting. I was dean, teaching a full load in a graduate school I had no associate dean a e time and also was in charge of the continuing education program. I was overcommitted and overworked. It would have been easy to say, "We did our best." and drop the program. However, I decided to teach the course myself. Faithfulness paid off. The first week, a very qualified young woman applied for the position. She did a great job teaching the course for five years determination and faith paid off.

It Is Easier to Keep Up Than to Catch Up

A bad habit undergraduates can get into is let their class assignments get behind, then "cram" for exams. This is such a bad habit I took the advice of Dr. George Gillen, ever-popular business professor at ORU, and gave pop quizzes to encourage students to keep up in their work. I strongly believe we all need to keep priorities straight, work on what is important, and not fall behind.

Luck Is the Idol of the Idle

Too many people put too much emphasis on luck. Opportunities are created by opportunistic people who do not sit back and wait for something to happen.

Working His Way Out of a Job

A good measure of the long-term effectiveness of a manager is the concept of working his way out of a job. The ultimate test of delegation is when key results are attained and people in the work unit are performing. In my entire career, the best example is Charles Triblcock, chairman and president of Liberty Industries. Liberty is prospering, has a well-developed strategic plan, a system to keep it on target, and a reward program tied to specific accountability of key

results. Triblcock guides the organization through delegated authority even while on annual European vacations, ski trips, and ten weeks in Florida. He is a role model for all of us.

There Are No Second Chances for Making a First Impression

People can only judge by what they see, read, and hear. The letter you mail, the way you answer the phone, and how you look all create an impression. That is a fact you cannot control. However, you can try to control the kind of impression you give. A well-written letter with no errors and on bond paper, a professional tone on the phone, and appropriate dress all help in making a good first impression. Many professional people conduct business over meals, and I have seen several lost opportunities because of sloppy dining habits.

Mother Teresa: A Life Not Dedicated to the Service of Mankind Is Useless

Mother Teresa has an interesting concept. IBM prominently uses the word "service" when discussing purpose and mission. The Lord has given all organizations and people certain gifts and strengths. If much is given, much is required. If we are all striving to serve mankind, the world can become a better place. We can all serve, through our professions and our personal lives.

Success Is Never Accidental

Often you hear, "He's lucky;' or "She got all the Breaks." But people make their own breaks. Success comes after hard work. I do not know of any successful person who got there by accident.

Never Ask Anyone to Do Something You Would Not Do Yourself

The late Roscoe Henry Channing, for whom I am named, was president of Hudson Bay Mining and Smelting Company from 1927 to 1968. He graduated from Princeton University in 1889 as a mining engineer, was on the first All-American football team, and was a rough rider with Teddy

Part II: Practical Applications of Common Sense Management

Roosevelt. Based on society's measure of success, I believe he made it.

Perhaps of equal importance was how he managed and dealt with people. He never asked a man to do anything he would not do himself. It is said that after an explosion once, the miners were afraid to go down and pick up the remains of a fellow miner blown to bits. Channing asked for volunteers - none came forward, so he, president of the company, put on work clothes and got a sack. He went down seven thousand feet into the mine by himself, picked up the remains, and brought them to the surface. He knew most of the four thousand employees by their first names and earned great respect from employees. There was but one strike in thirty years. He was ahead of his time, offering fringe benefits, free hospitalizations, vacations, things unknown in other mines at that time in Canada. He had flowers and plants in the mine building. It was a spotless building, on the theory that since men spend a third of their lives working, they should work in pleasant surroundings. All of Channing's mines were the height of efficiency -always built on hillsides to take advantage of gravity and reduce power usage. The mine never missed a dividend during R. Henry Channing's tenure of management.

The Fellow Pulling the Oars Has Little Time to Rock the Boat

Have you noticed the loudest complainers are usually people not involved in the work? The key is that the manager must involve his key people in the plan and get them working on its execution. If people are "pulling oars," they will not be "rocking the boat."

Conclusion

The purpose of *Common Sense Management – A Biblical Perspective* is to bridge the gap between the theory of management and the application of that theory.

This book attempts to help us all be better managers. As we lead and manage, we face many different, complex situations. I hope that after reading and reflecting on this book, when you confront one of these situations, some of the principles in the book, such as "Care and Feeding . . .," "Iceberg," and so forth, will flash into your mind and help you determine the best course of action.

Common Sense Management -A Biblical Perspective also illuminates the truth that most of managing and leading is common sense.

The study of the Bible shows us that these principles have a source and have been here since the beginning of time. *Common Sense Management -A Biblical Perspective* is a supplement to the Bible. When mixed together, both books can help you become what God has a vision for you to be, what He knows you can be.

Part II: Practical Applications of Common Sense Management

Appendix A

Other "Common Sense" Quotes

> REMEMBER THIS YOUR LIFETIME THROUGH –
> TOMORROW, THERE WILL BE MORE TO DO . . .
> AND FAILUDRE WAITS FOR ALL WHO STAY,
> WITH SOME SUCCESS MADE YESTERDAY . . .
> TOMORROW, YOU MUST TRY ONCE· MORE,
> AND EVEN HARDER THAN BEFORE.[4]
> —John Wooden

Do not let what you cannot do interfere with what you can do.
He who knows little soon tells it.
If you are content with the best you have done,
You will never do the best you can do.
You drift toward the rocks, you row toward success.
The best place to find a helping hand is at the end of your arm.
When you are through improving -you are through.
If you do not know where you are going, any road will take you there.

---

[4] Wooden, John.

Common Sense Management—A Biblical Perspective

> Every great and commanding movement in the annals of the world is the triumph of enthusiasm Nothing great was ever achieved without it.[5]
>
> —Ralph Waldo Emerson

> Talent is God-given, be humble.
> Fame is man-given, be thankful.
> Conceit is self-given, be careful.

> Whatever impedes a man, but does not stop him, aids his progress.
> Having fun is doing hard things well.
> Set a goal -then get rid of those things in your life that keep you from attaining that goal.
> There is just one discouraging thing about the rules of success:
> They will not work unless we do.
> The doctrine of chances is the Bible of the fool.[6]
>
> —William Gilmore Simms

> Consider the hammer:
> It does not lose its head until it flies off the handle.
> You cannot win a heavyweight title by doing lightweight exercises.

---

[5] Brown, Ralph Emerson, ed. The New Dictionary of Thoughts (Standard Book Company, 1965), p. 176.
[6] Ibid. p. 77.

Part II: Practical Applications of Common Sense Management

A chip on the shoulder indicates wood higher up.

The trouble with being a good sport
Is that you have to lose to be one.

Beware of a half-truth -you may be getting the wrong half.

Success comes from hanging on after all others have let go.

A hard fall means a high bounce
if you are made of the right material.

Even a mosquito does not get a slap on the back
until he starts working.

It is nice to be important, but it is important to be nice.

When you get to the end of your hope, Tie a knot, and hang on.

When yesterday's deeds still look good today,
Then you have not done much today,

Great minds discuss ideas, small minds discuss people.

What you are to be, you are now becoming.

It is usually uphill work that lands one on top.

A mob has many heads, but no brains.

If you do not know where you are going, you will never know if, or when, you get there.

Forever the dream is in the mind, realization is in the hand.

The courageous are those who reach.

NOT WHERE I'M SUPPOSED TO BE,
I'M NOT WHAT I WANT TO BE,
BUT I'M NOT WHAT I USED TO BE.
I HAVEN'T LEARNED HOW TO ARRIVE,
I'VE JUST LEARNED HOW TO KEEP ON GOING.

The harder you work, the harder it is to surrender.

Do not count the days, make the days count.

A person is not a failure as long as he keeps trying.
It is when he stops trying that he becomes a failure.

Sometimes you have to look hard at a person and remember . . .

Part II: Practical Applications of Common Sense Management

He is just trying to get some place . . . just like you.
What a man is depends largely on what he does when he has nothing to do.
The man with time to burn never gave the world Any light.

BE CAREFUL OF THE WORDS YOU SAY
SO KEEP THEM SOFT AND SWEET.
YOU NEVER KNOW FROM DAY TO DAY
WHICH ONES YOU'LL HAVE TO EAT.[7]
—Marcus Allen

The lazy man aims at nothing -and generally hits it.
A turtle never makes progress until he sticks out his neck.
If your work speaks for itself, then do not interrupt it.
You cannot fly with the owls at night and expect to soar with the eagles during the day.
The one who complains about the way the ball bounces is likely the one who dropped it.
Usually the guy who blows his horn loudest is in the biggest fog.
Do not look back unless you plan to go that way.
God does not promise us a trouble-free journey— only a safe arrival.
Lead, follow, or get out of the way.[8]

---

[7] Allen, Marcus. Los Angeles Raiders

Common Sense Management—A Biblical Perspective

—George Steinbrenner

If it is to be, it is up to me.

Get the tide up, and all the boats will rise.

Assets: Make things possible.

People: Make things happen.

Learn as if you were to live forever.

Live as if you were to die tomorrow.

You cannot live a perfect day without doing something.

For someone who will never be able to repay you. It is what you learn after you know it all that counts.

If you do not stand up for something, you will fall for anything. Ability may get you to the top, but it takes character to keep you there.

You may be at the top of the heap, but you are still part of it. Ham and eggs: The chicken is involved, but the hog is committed. Muscles do not produce net profit. Laugh and the world laughs with you. Weep, and you weep alone.[9]

—Ella Wheeler Wilcox

You have not failed until you start blaming someone else.

---

[8] Steinbrunner, George. Owner of the New York Yankees.
[9] Wilcox, Ella Wheeler. The Oxford Dictionary of Quotations (Oxford University Press, Amen House, London E.C. 4, Second Edition, 1955), p. 568:26.

Part II: Practical Applications of Common Sense Management

Appendix B

"Common Sense Quotes from Scripture"

Purpose/Mission/Vision

Proverbs 11:14: "For lack of guidance a nation (or in our case 'a person') falls, but many advisers make victory sure." (NIV)

Proverbs 15:22: "Plans fail for lack of counsel, but with many advisers they succeed." (NIV)

Proverbs 20:18: "Every purpose is established by counsel ... ."

Proverbs 16:20: "He that handleth a matter wisely shall find good . . . ."

Proverbs 29:18: 'Where there is no vision, the people perish . . ."

Proverbs 23:7: "As a man thinketh in his heart, so is he" (paraphrased).

Joel 2:28: ". . . your old men shall dream dreams, your young men shall see visions."

Acts 2:17: (Essentially the same as Joel 2:28.)

Romans 12:3: "For by the grace given me I say to every one of you: Do not think of yourself more highly than you ought, but rather think of yourself with sober judgment, in

Part II: Practical Applications of Common Sense Management

accordance with the measure of faith God has given you:' (NIV)

Galatians 6:3-4: "If anyone thinks he is something when he is nothing, he himself. Each one should test his own actions. Then he can take pride in himself, without comparing himself to somebody else . . . " (NIV)

Ephesians 4:1: ". . . I urge you to live a life worthy of the calling you have received" (NIV).

Psalm 37:4: "Delight yourself in the Lord and he will give you the desires of your heart" (NIV).

Matthew 6:33: "But seek first his kingdom and his righteousness, and all these things will be given to you as well" (NIV).

Strengths and Weaknesses

Luke 12:48: "To whom much is given, much is" (paraphrased).

2 Timothy 3:17: ". . . complete and proficient, well-fitted and thoroughly equipped for every good work" (AMP).

Strategy

Matthew 5:15: "Neither do people light a lamp and put it under a bowl. Instead they put it on its stand, and it gives light to everyone in the house" (paraphrased).

Operational Plan

2 Timothy 2:15	"Study to shew thyself approved Unto God, a workman that needeth not to be ashamed …."
2 Timothy 3:17:	"… complete and proficient, well-Fitted and thoroughly equipped for Every good work" (AMP).
Luke 14:28:	"For which one of you when he wants to build a tower does not sit down and calculate the cost?" (paraphrased).
Philippians 4:13:	"I can do all things through Christ Which strengtheneth me."
Colossians 3:17:"	and whatsoever we do in word or deed, do all in the name of the Lord Jesus …."
Proverbs 16:9:	"We should make plans – counting On God to direct us." (TLB)
Proverbs 16:3:	"Commit thy works unto the Lord."
Colossians 3:23:	"Whatever you do, work at it with all Your heart, as working for the Lord, not for men" (NIV).
Nehemiah 2:4:	"The king said to me, 'What is it you want?' Then I prayed to the God of heaven,"

Plan in General

Part II: Practical Applications of Common Sense Management

Proverbs 15:22: "Plans fail for lack of counsel, but with many advisers they succeed" (NIV).

Proverbs *16:10:* "A divine sentence is in the lips of the king: his mouth transgresseth not in judgment."

Proverbs *19:20:* "Hear counsel, and receive instruction, that thou mayest be wise. . ."

Proverbs 20:5: "A plan in the heart of a man is like deep water" (paraphrased).

Proverbs 24:3: "Through wisdom is a house built, And by understanding it is established."

1 Corinthians 14:33: "For God is not the author of confusion, but of peace . . . "

Reward

1 Corinthians *3:8:* "Now he who plants and he who waters are one; but each will receive his own reward according to his own labor" (paraphrased).

Proverbs 13:21 "The righteous will be rewarded with prosperity" (paraphrased).

Philippians 3:14: "I press toward the mark for the prize of the high calling of God in Christ

Jesus."

Part II: Practical Applications of Common Sense Management

Part III: Readings
"Point of View"
by R. Henry Migliore

Part III: Readings

"Point of View"

Some Keys to Business Survival

We appear to have reached a point in the chronology of America that has placed both organizational and individual lives in precarious and often crisis positions. Corporations, as well as individuals, are failing and taking bankruptcy. Many people are floundering as they seek new career opportunities and readjust their lives.

Over the past twenty years, I have learned a management philosophy and way of thinking that can provide direction based on observing successful organizations and people in these organizations:

Identify the specific needs of the organization in terms of key result areas.

Identify specific needs of the persons in the organization. These are usually self-esteem, recognition, and the opportunity for independent thought and action -based on longitudinal surveys we have conducted over the past ten years.

Have the organizational team work together, emphasizing the process of planning to determine where the organization wants to be in five years.

To determine where it wants to be in five years, the management group must identify purpose, conduct environmental analysis, assess strengths and weaknesses and make assumptions. This creates a written product of their efforts, a plan in writing.

Common Sense Management—A Biblical Perspective

After completing assessment of these steps, both individuals and the group must set specific key objectives for the fifth year.

Working back from the fifth year, the organization determines what it wants to accomplish the fourth, third, second, and first years.

If next year's accomplishments do not meet with reality based on the present situation, then the organization must redefine what is possible next year and work through to the fifth year, seeking compromises each step of the way.

Strategies for achieving these objectives must be determined. Every organizational member should have an opportunity to contribute to these strategies.

This plan is still considered to be a rough-draft stage until it is presented to whatever is considered the next highest level of management or group to which the management group reports. This gets everything out in the open and is the first step in recognizing the difference between expectations and reality. It is most important that what is to be accomplished, and how, is agreed upon before the task begins.

Once the overall five-year plan and strategy are agreed upon, the organization is set to go into action.

Operational and action plans are started with an emphasis on breaking down every key result area, making certain persons responsible for the completion of every activity, and clearly defining the authority for every short-term task.

Part III: Readings

A system of reporting success and failure must be determined so that every step from the action steps through-the implementation of long- term overall strategies can be identified.

Any organizational member should be able to signal a deviation from the plan that requires immediate action to get back on target.

A system of intrinsic and extrinsic rewards must be established to reward the organization and provide reinforcement as it goes about the task of getting where it wants to be.

These overall steps will ensure success for an organization or individual. I am continually reminded, and see evidence, that those following this process have met with a large measure of success. It takes hard work, time, and dedication to adhere to a management philosophy and use the strategic planning steps.

The key points are to determine where you want to be in the long term, involve as many people as possible in planning, set targets along the way, provide timely accurate feedback as you progress, and then provide rewards when the right things happen.

[Reprinted from Tahlequah Daily Press, Sunday, September 20, 1987, p. 6A.]

Common Sense Management—A Biblical Perspective

"Point of View"

Twenty Sure Ways to Lose Money

After twenty years of helping people solve business and personal problems, I have discovered a few ways to lose one's hard-earned money. Listen carefully for these phrases, and your objective will soon be attained:

- This opportunity is available for only a short time . .
- You have been selected as a winner of a fabulous prize. You must . . .
- All your friends are in on this . . . .
- You have earned the right, through your success, to be considered for . . . .
- I am a (Christian, member of a lodge or club, and so forth). Do business with me . . .

Keep talking to the person who has this opening line and soon he will have, as the popular country song says, "the gold mine, and you will have the shaft."

Here are some rules to consider if your aim is to lose your money quickly:

1. Let someone else, preferably someone you do not know, bring you the investment idea. If they come to your door, by all means, let them in.
2. Constantly worry and plot against paying taxes. Find ways to lose so that you can deduct the losses from your taxes.

Part III: Readings

3. Be a recognized professional with your name in the yellow pages, such as a doctor or a dentist.
4. Be arrogant and have a "godlike" air.
5. Try to get rich quickly.
6. For the ultimate experience, invest money you cannot afford to lose.
7. Respond quickly with action when your mate says, "Why don't you do as well as ?"
8. Give your mate and children credit cards and no budget.
9. Send your children to college with no accountability. Provide a car, if possible. Keep them in college no matter what.
10. Use the phone and save those letters, postcards, and stamps.
11. Buy raw land, the farther away from home, the better.
12. Build your wife a bigger closet.
13. Go into a business you know nothing about.
14. Do not develop a personal life plan, a financial plan, or set goals.
15. Do not buy insurance of any kind.
16. Do not make out your own personal will. Watch your loved ones from Heaven while they fight over your estate and give most of it to lawyers.
17. Get a divorce.
18. Do a lot of impulse buying.
19. Keep all your money for yourself. Do not give to your church or any worthy cause.
20. Do not ask for any advice from professionals in banking, insurance, law, investments, and accounting.

Common Sense Management—A Biblical Perspective

This column is meant to make all of us think before we spend. We all have most likely made some poor economic decisions and learned good lessons. Our quality of life can be affected by our economic decisions. It is to be hoped that we will be more careful and think through how we invest and spend our money.

[Reprinted by permission of The Tulsa Tribune from its August 21, 1987, issue.]

Part III: Readings

"Point of View"

Our "Rain Forests" Are Still Shifting

It appears our present society is facing the same problems dinosaurs faced eons ago.

The dinosaurs were gigantic animals that lived mostly in and around water. Their habitat was rivers and swamps, and they ate soft water plants. Perhaps over thousands of years, the rain forests shifted, and dinosaurs were unable to adapt to a new environment, which--I am speculating--might have become drier. The dinosaur did not survive and became extinct. Some plants, such as the cactus, and some other animals, such as the smaller lizards, were able to adapt and survive. Still other animals, fish, and birds followed the rain forests and survived.

It appears our society is facing the same kind of shifting that the dinosaurs faced millions of years ago. Some who can continue to live by the same plans and strategies will be able to adapt and survive as the lizard and the cactus did. Other organizations and people will recognize the shift, change and adapt, and keep their activities meeting the needs. of people in the mainstream of a shifting world. These organizations and people will prosper.

In northeastern Oklahoma, there are some recognizable trends already:

1) Oil and farm economies continue to decline, 2) tourism is receiving a stronger emphasis, 3) NSU is assuming greater prominence as an educational and cultural center, 4) people are

Common Sense Management—A Biblical Perspective
recognizing that the quality of our water and air must be protected, and 5) the region is becoming a more and more popular retirement area.

All the residents of this area would like to keep things just as they are -the dinosaurs would have preferred the rain forests not to shift. However, we must recognize that this entire exciting, problematical, often frustrating and anxiety-filled world in which we live is experiencing a great wave of change.

We need to acknowledge change and try to adapt as the changes take place. It makes little sense to stay as we are. Past experiences will not be as good a predictor as they have been. It will be of more importance to recognize the rate of change and the direction the world is taking.

[Reprinted by permission of the Tahlequah Daily Press, from its Sunday, October 25, 1987, issue.]

Part III: Readings

"Point of View"

A Look Toward the Year 2000 and the Year 2001

In one of my columns, published in August, 1987, I predicted three major occurrences by the year 2000—based on the fact that it is easier to predict changes of great magnitude will take place than to pinpoint when those changes will take place.

A futurist can say there will be upheavals, highs and lows, political instability, wars and rumors of wars. Those general predictions are relatively easy because they reflect man and how he has conducted his affairs through the centuries. My three predictions were:

1. We know that something unpredictable and dramatic is going to take place by the year 1990.
2. Look for political uncertainty. There are any number of "hot" spots, including Iran, that will create a chain effect that will ripple to the year 2000.
3. Over the next fifteen years, we can count on a major economic high and a major low. Again, no one can predict when either will happen.

I then concluded that all of us must be ready to cope and to react to a quickly changing world. Who would have predicted a space shuttle disaster, an air attack on Libya, or a nuclear disaster in the Soviet Union? To me, these events are prima facie evidence we can count on more of the same.

Let's look at those three things and speculate further:

1. Perhaps the three events could have been predicted now that we know the facts surrounding their occurrence, but something even more unpredictable is coming.
2. Add Libya to the original list, and be ready.
3. We are searching for the economic high. Anyone who doubts that "what goes up, comes down; needs only to refresh his memory with the prices of oil, gold, and silver. I believe the stock market is in a period of adjustment and bears watching.

In conclusion, do not panic! Look at the horizon. Do not get caught napping. Look at the great opportunities. Adapt when the world changes and do more than just survive in this ever-changing world. Live life to the fullest.

Part III: Readings

"Point of View"

Key Plays in the Game of Life

The difference between the winner of the PGA Gold Tourney and the tenth player is an average of one stroke, the fiftieth player only four strokes. You have to be a really good golfer to even be in the top two hundred, but a margin of only six strokes separates the top player from the two hundredth player.

In a study of aerodynamics, one learns that the leading portion of the wing provides most of an airplane's lift. Of all the square feet of space in the plane, only this very small area up and down each wing provides the margin to lift the plane.

The launching of the Columbia spaceship was an intricate maneuver. Everything had to be exact in terms of the centrifugal force of the earth's movement, the launching speed, and the power as the spaceship is thrust into space. The slightest margin of error on the launch will cause the spaceship to be off hundreds of thousands of miles as it goes into orbit.

Everyone enjoyed the NCAA basketball champion ship playoff a few years ago between Georgetown and North Carolina. The teams played shot-for-shot and point-far-point for forty minutes. With sixteen seconds to go, and Georgetown behind by one point, the final play of the game was the margin of difference between being the NCAA champion and finishing in second

place.

Common Sense Management—A Biblical Perspective

If you study a football game, you will find that five or six key plays make the difference in the game. If the coaches knew which plays these would be, they would practice all week on those particular plays to be sure they were executed perfectly. The problem is that out of the eighty to one hundred plays executed, coaches do not know in advance which will be the key plays. This forces players to execute all of the plays with precision so that six or seven are executed properly. The margin for winning boils down to a very few plays.

The difference between winning and losing in our lives can be fulfilled in the margin. Whenever the marginal play comes along, if we are prepared to excel, we can become all that we can be.

As much as we want to think of something as glamorous and fascinating, there is always a "nitty- gritty" side that we have not seen. The most precious gem was once buried in dirt. To be truly beautiful it had to be polished, cut, and set in the right light. In its original state, it was just as worthy, but its full potential was not known until someone recognized it and was willing enough and patient to set it free.

The right amount of polishing is needed for you to realize your potential. It is not necessarily what you see on the outside that makes anyone or anything a beauty. It is that glow on the inside. There is always work to be done, a need to keep on refining, polishing, and simplifying. Continue to emphasize those things you learn as you continue to refine and polish your life.

We owe it to ourselves to bring out the best of who we are -to use our talents for something beautiful and worthy. That requires a staying power that comes only with vision and determination.

You need a plan. Here are the essential steps: Have a vision-dream, get the facts, be aware of what is going on around you, analyze your strengths and weaknesses, make a few assumptions, set definite measurable objectives, develop a list of strategies for each objective, put plan into action, review progress, and reward yourself for accomplishment.

R. HENRY MIGLIORE, PhD, is a leading strategist for long-term planning for business, sports, and religious leaders. He offers consulting services as well as resources including books, videos, articles, seminars, and training sessions.

He is currently the president of Managing for Success, an international consulting company. Dr. Migliore teaches at the graduate and undergraduate levels at universities worldwide. He was Professor of Management and former Dean of the ORU School of Business from 1975 until 1987. From 1887 to 2003 he was Facet Enterprises Professor of Management at UCT/'NSU Tulsa. From 2003 to date he has worked worldwide as author, visiting professor and consultant. He is currently assisting ORU Global Outreach Center with broadcasts to various target markets worldwide.

He is a former manager of the press manufacturing operations of the Continental Can Company's Stockyard Plant. Prior to that he was responsible for the industrial engineering function at Continental's Indiana plant. In this capacity, Dr. Migliore was responsible for coordinating the long-range planning process. In addition, he has had various consulting experiences with Fred Rudge & Associates in New York and has served large and small businesses, associations, and non-profit organizations in various capacities.

He has made presentations to a wide variety of clubs, groups, and professional associations. Dr. Migliore has been selected to be on the faculty for the International Conferences on Management by Objectives and Strategic Planning Institute Seminar Series and he is a frequent contributor to the Academy of Management. He served for 12 years on the Board of Directors of T.D. Williamson, Inc., and was previously on the Boards of the International MBO Institute and Brush Creek Ranch, American Red Cross/Tulsa Chapter, and is chairman of a scholarship fund for Eastern State College. In 1984, he was elected into the Eastern State College Athletic Hall of Fame. Dr. Migliore has been a guest lecturer on a number of college campuses, including Harvard, Texas A&M, Pepperdine, ITESM, Guadalajara, Autonoma De Guadalajara, and University of Calgary Executive Development programs. He serves on many chamber and civic committees. He was selected Who's Who on a list of 31 top echelon writers and consultants in America.

Dr. Migliore's books have been translated into Russian, Chinese, Korean, Spanish, German, and Japanese.

He has 17 books in total. His next book in process is *Fourth Quarter Redefined*.

R. HENRY MIGLIORE, PhD
PRESIDENT OF MANAGING FOR SUCCESS
10839 SOUTH HOUSTON • JENKS, OK 74037 • (918) 299-0007

EMAIL: HMIGLIORE@AOL.COM
WEBSITE: WWW.HMIGLIORE.COM • YOUTUBE: DRMIGLIORE

www.ingramcontent.com/pod-product-compliance
Lightning Source LLC
LaVergne TN
LVHW051607070426
835507LV00021B/2810